Furry Tales

Jude Aquilina

Furry Tales

Furry Tales
ISBN 978 1 74027 923 9
Copyright © text Jude Aquilina 2015
Copyright © images Angelee Theodoros 2015

First published 2015 by
GINNINDERRA PRESS
PO Box 3461 Port Adelaide 5015 Australia
www.ginninderrapress.com.au

Contents

Imagine the First Cat in England	9
Cat in a Blue Boat	11
Lullabies	13
B C	14
Mr Piecroft	15
Old Cat	17
Careers for Cats	19
Panthera	21
Of Mice and Leaves	23
Mouse Plague	25
Portrait of Man and Cat	26
In Season	27
Of Ink and Life	29
Lunar Cat	31
Prowlers	32
Magill Grain Store	33
Dark Garden	35
Circus of Cats	37
Flea Hunting	39
King Gussie	41
Paper Bags	43
Outcast	45
The Well	46
Invisible Visitor	47
Shape-shifters	49
Mog or Dog?	50
Felis Domestica	51
Acknowledgements	53

This book is dedicated to my feline friends

Bobby, Frosty, Biggie and Stinkrat,

and to the memory of Mr Piecroft

The widow's cat keeps warmer than the bride's.
— Fazil Hüsnü Dağlarca

Imagine the First Cat in England

Imagine the first *felis domestica*, unloaded onto a bustling pier. Perhaps it hissed – or purred – to be on solid ground. Imagine seeing it released in a dusty warehouse, walking like liquid velvet, its sheen catching rays of wan sun – then, ears a-twitch, flattening out on its haunches with a rear-end wiggle, like an athlete at the starting line. Imagine the surprise when it leaps and pounces faster than human comprehension, then struts back, growling and proud, showing onlookers a rat, dragged by the neck, droplets of blood beading its path. Imagine this gift placed at your feet, then after a rub and a sawmill purr, the stripy hero is back on guard, till the shed is vermin-free. Imagine everyone wanting one of these little hunters that crunches bones then settles on a cosy lap, to sleep and twitch with dreams.

Imagine later, when cats burrowed deep into the English psyche and beds, replacing warming pans and shrinks; they entertained young and old; some even sat in prams wearing bonnets and bows. They took care of scraps and sour milk, and emptied goldfish ponds. Imagine their annual small gifts, delivered in haystacks: little blind sacks of fur, kneading their mothers' bellies. Eventually, cats starred in plays and books and found their place in high society: that is, until the Inquisition deemed black cats evil and burned or drowned them with their witches. Imagine the English feline, like the countryman, sharing unjust poverty and persecution, though remaining stoic, getting on with living and loving, even migrating to the antipodes.

Cat in a Blue Boat

Tabby captain, stripes wrinkly
as the rippling Mediterranean,
who taught you stinky fish?
Who said it'd be worth the salty
tail and stiffened whiskers
to perch up on the prow,
prouder than any angler
returning with a bumper catch?

Apart from the purring that starts
well before the nets are gathered in,
have you other shanties to share?
Does your good luck legend
make you figurehead, mascot
and ally, and ensure you
are appeased with mullet,
whiting, salmon and trevally?

When sun sets, and you leave
your dusky, liquid hunting ground,
retract your sharp, white hooks,
do you seek out a silky moon of milk?
Does some kindly villager
let you lick-wash on their porch
then doze among pots of red geraniums
away from the grip of cruel Boreas?

Lullabies

for Max Fatchen

Like a ticking clock to an orphaned cat
the tinkle of rain on a tin roof
takes me back to my first bedroom:
a corrugated-iron lean-to
where wind thrummed through louvres
and the moon was a comfort
peeping through a curtain of clouds.

Curling myself around a hot water bottle
with Sally the tabby anchored at my feet,
I perfected the game of shadows
seeing faces and wings as wide as eagles'
sweeping past my window;
under the streetlight's yellow fog
castles grew, and morphing beasts
sneered from behind the bare branches.

A shy child, fearful of the dark,
these rhythms kept me safe –
the pulse beats of a clock, the hum of purrs
and whoosh of steady rain.
Even now, I lie awake to listen,
in this era of tiled roofs and digital time
and pine for those past lullabies,
grateful for the murmurings of my moggy.

B C*

My windows have websites
with real, not virtual, spiders.
They will inject more than ink
into my scream if I try to delete
with bare fingers.
My laptop is a cat, her paws
the only pads a mouse encounters
in this house.

* Before Computer

Mr Piecroft

Mr Piecroft is the kind of cat
that needs a lot of pats.
If I stand with my back to a chair,
he's likely to climb up on my shoulder,
little skin-pricking barbs latching on,
chin nudging my cheek, till I sit,
then he plops onto my knee,
purring contentedly.

The ideal captain's companion
on a long sea journey, he'd be sleeping
on deck despite the roll and pitch,
on duty each evening, protecting the larder
or sharing his softness evenly
between laps and legs of homesick crew.
At port, he'd relish fresh milk
and guard the anchor chain
against stowaway rats.

My friends call him 'the greeting cat',
for no one enters my front gate
without this white S-bend stalling their stride,
meowing and escorting them to my door.
If he were tiger-size, he'd ask them to climb aboard.
If he was human he'd carry their bags
and pour them a martini before introductions,
even the Mormons are heralded as kings
well before their bike wheels have stopped spinning.

Old Cat

Is poem about old cat I once had / I call old one Stinkrat / he live to shaggy twenty / is poem of purr-engine cat / the sort that sit and rub and rub and nibble till you give ear-rubble then he roll on back / if no scratch / he scratch / you must tummy-tickle rough and round and up and down and he purr and purr / and when you stop he stand up and head-butt / purring louder / louder / if no more come he swipe leg or he clamber up and bite pen / no more writing he say pushing big skull up under my chin / he bad old ankle-nipping cat when food take too long / he hiss-snake cat when tread on tail / he sneak and steal from table cat but when I look he just clean paw beside empty pie / he bad and he old / and I'll be that one day / so I open can for toothless yowl and pat scruffy head.

Careers for Cats

This creative creature is highly skilled,
capable of working in many fields…
employed as bird scarers for fruiting trees,
foot warmers and cures for arthritic knees,
roofing inspectors and armchair minders
fireside fixtures and wool unwinders.
In midnight soirees, they're found in clusters
of yodellers, divas and backstreet buskers;

They'll mop up spilt milk, and polish your shins
taste-test all your food as epicureans;
they speak the language of motors and snakes,
guard your front doors and make good bedspread weights.
They'll knead pillows till all the lumps are gone;
with paws full of hooks, will fish out your pond.

They're window watchers and vermin gnawers
fridge door sentries, cardboard box explorers,
teachers of meditation and of sound sleep
sensors of sunshine and electric heat,
magnets for dogs and spring-loaded mousetraps
security guards for unwelcome cats;
and although they'll often take leave to roam
they'll transform any house into a home.

Panthera

That's my cat,
mean, black, muscular
a flow of molasses
a dart of night through day
sculptured onyx
like a statue
at a king's door
curved spine
perfect as any
Pythagorean arc.

Mocking her
risks a raking;
laughing
yields furrowed flesh
and don't try to comb
or tummy-rubble –
this Cleopatra
dispatches asps
and every other cat
on her patch.

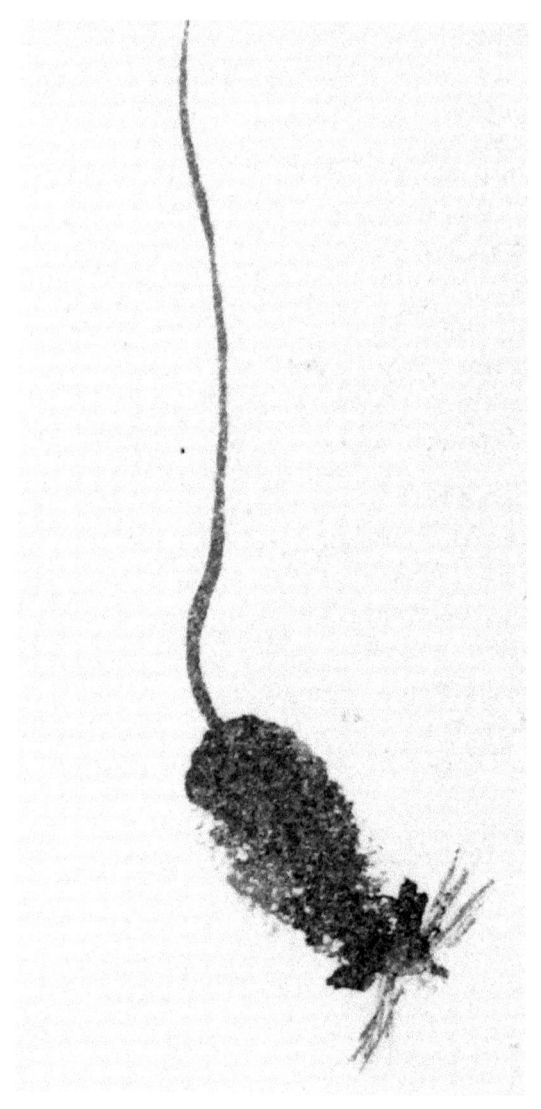

Of Mice and Leaves

My cat, Frosty, loves autumn,
all those flat mice spiralling down
from walnut trees. Pouncing paws
snap their crunchy tails

as he springs up to greet
each falling body, back-flipping
and frisking like a lamb
in a field of orange and brown.

Each year, he attacks
this deciduous plague
with renewed vigour,
sporting from dawn till dinner.

Now and then, he captures
a real, live, furry parcel
and carries it in his mouth,
alerting us with a low growl.

This one's mine. I'm not sharing,
he implies. Then, like a child
with a hacky-sack, he juggles
and whacks his new toy.

He's visibly low in winter
sprawled by the fire, head on paws;
I'm certain that he's dreaming
of autumn sun and showers of mice.

Mouse Plague

Mid-north, South Australia, 1980

The road, a seething carpet
of tiny, furry pelts, some flat,
most moving, scouring
for skerricks of food.

We empty kitchen bins,
breaking up mouse parties within;
cupboard corners are plugged
with steel wool, yet still
they burrow into our lives.

Tail flicking, the cat sits aloft
like a child locked in a lolly shop
with a bellyache. Too much
of any food is nauseous.

A water-filled 44-gallon drum
with slippery footbridge
and smelly salami
hung just out of reach
yields buckets of soggy bodies.

After breaking rains arrive
gutters flow with leaves and mice
and a week of hoary dawns
marks the end of pestilence.
Now, the cat at least raises her head
when a survivor skitters by.

Portrait of Man and Cat

When frost beards diamond panes
the black cat glows ferrous orange
in the light of the open fire that spits
and hisses at this best-chair usurper.

And an elderly man lowers an empty bottle
his red whiskers and nose also aglow;
he swears and croons snippets of songs
then sprawls out asleep on the tabletop.

Out cold, the fire dies, the cat stirs
as bitter wind licks under the door.
The man wakes, mumbles a threat
at the cat licking his dinner plate.

Once the next log takes off,
the still life resumes, each subject
back in their place in the dim lit frame
until morning stirs their empty bellies.

In Season

Awakened by a yodelled scream.
I sit bolt upright, as does my female kitten
who howls back in a higher pitch.
The baritone tom responds
in wild verses of caterwauls,
enough to wake the deaf from death:
a John Cage experiment in melodious discord.

Then my old neutered cat raises his paw
and swipes the upturned rear of the striped kitten.
It's as if he's saying, 'snap out of it, sister,
you'll regret it in the morning…' Love is fickle
as frost, it glows and sparkles, but soon melts
and leaves you burnt and swollen with regret.

Of ink and life

What difference between plate and lake
when a swan floats upon the glassy surface?
The minds and fingers of artists and calligraphers
know tide lines, reeds, the graceful arc of flight –
the uplift and sinuous sweep of muscle and wing;
the ovum curve of bird's breast in morning light.
Two quick brushstrokes and a swallow is born,
dash of beak and it lives on a page of white sky.
Then a cat curls into sleep, three whisker flicks
and the black line breathes on a parchment rug.
The great masters recreated sacred images
learnt from God's geometry, nature's symmetry
to flesh the hollow bones of Aves and angels.

Lunar Cat

The luminous amber gems
of the cat's eyes
flash at midnight, fastening
a long lighthouse gaze
on the mother-of-pearl
moon floating gently
on her sea of rippled cloud.

Prowlers

One sounds like a witchdoctor/wolf
howling, growling in guttural tones;
the other, a helpless child, whining,
whimpering, pleading to go home.
They speak in tongues below my window.
Cats or demons? Do they know I'm in the bath
rigor mortis stiff and breathing softly?

Closer they chant their evil voodoo
luring me up to the foggy glass
but the scene is shrouded in silence:
nothing but leaves, enchantingly still
so I sink to warmth and hair-washing,
but just when I'm under, rinsing conditioner
a scream vibrates through iron and water.

I surface, dripping like the living dead
my heart a frantic bongo drum
my mind a mosaic of horror movies.
This is no way to enjoy my bath:
straining ears, shivering shoulders.
I find the courage to pull the plug
leave on the strength of the gurgle.

Magill Grain Store

En route to school, I'd proffer two cents
for a small paper bag of wheat to chew.
The grey-coated men with powdery hands
always asked after my fantail pigeons.
Now, forty years on: the same hay dust scent
and tortoiseshell cat, sphinx-like on a sack
of Happy Hen laying pellets;
sibilant sluices of grain pour from metal chutes
like streams of soup; dust clouds cut as hatches shut.

The backdrop straw fortress is often decorated
with mewing kittens. A fine lace of webs
bedecks crowns of cuttlefish hanging over a cluster
of brown bottles called Iodine and Lice Rid.
Stacked to the power of ten,
plump hessian bags ascend like a giant abacus.
In every corner, little blue pools
of poison to capture what the cats miss.

From eight to five, an endless tide
of utilities and station wagons surges through
the iron lean-to. Then, boots agape, trailing straw,
customers merge with the flow of upper Magill Road,
to return to their feathered companions
with another few month's fodder. I like to stand
on the landing and breathe it all in…one day
I might ask again if I can stick my hand
into a wheat bin and take a ginger kitten home.

Dark Garden

A lover of crows and all things black, I grew pansies, their pitch cheeks and yellow eyes like little tigers in the moonlight. Then I planted a patch of monkshood, their humble heads cowled in brown, cosseted by leaves, poison tongued. Black-eyed Susan overruns my garage, housing a hundred huntsmen spiders under her skirt. Black Jack zucchini have staked out the vegie patch, begun weapons production.

I buried devil's lilies, that later sprouted and bloomed, tall and caped with obscene scarlet stamens and secret bulbous chambers oozing the stench of rotten meat. At first, I searched for a carcass, till eventually I sniffed out the source: harlot of the Arum family, her pong's purpose to lure bejewelled blowflies into a sticky belly to become her pollinating slaves. My mother shakes her head at my morbid garden and my black tom cat, who likes splashing around his own cologne. But good luck hums with his purr as he licks my stress away – and at night he fights like a phantom, keeping the pale strays at bay.

Circus of Cats

Down by the River Moggy on the grassy flats
They are setting up tents for the Circus of Cats.
The locals are making an excited beeline
to witness this troupe of acrobatic felines.
The word is out that these clever cats dance and sing,
juggle mice and rats and jump through flaming rings.

The audience is cheering and making a din
as the ringmaster bows and all the cats file in,
led by a fat-headed mangy old ginger tom
who jumps on command and beats a brass gong.
Next comes a lean and haughty, fluffy white Persian
dancing the tango in a four-legged version.

The ringmaster places ten hurdles in a row,
cries, 'Now watch what happens on my whistle blow.'
But before his painted lips can tickle the reed,
a sleek, black cat has backed up and taken the lead.
It sprays his satin trousers and swipes at his shin
then climbs up to the trapeze and begins to swing.

The audience is deafening with loud applause
as a shabby tabby climbs him with unsheathed claws
paws off his curly wig and swings it through the air
then scampers off up the aisle with her prize of hair;
she jumps on an old lady and begins to dance
causing her to swear and bellow and wet her pants.

The circus tent is echoing with children's screams
because the cats have stolen all of their ice creams.
Then the ringmaster shouts and tries to reign them in
but the big ginger tom takes a stockwhip to him,
howling, 'You should know that cats cannot be herded.
Now jump through this fiery ring before you're murdered!'

And the last the crowd saw of that old ringmaster
was in Moggy River swimming from their laughter.
And the moral of this story spread even faster:
Always remember the cat is the master!

Flea Hunting

In the days before flea collars
our old tabby tom would let
eccentric Aunt Nan inspect him.
Her long red fingernails
parted stripes and fur.
She'd talk to him:
'There's one.'
'Stay still.'
'Yes!'
and we'd hear the satisfying click
as she squished
a reddish-black flea
between thumbnails.

This cat scratched most people
but, like a bison with a tick-picking
bird, he knew that Aunt Nan's
sport was good for him.

King Gussie

The old tomcat's tail appeared at the window,
like a paintbrush gone stiff in jellied turps.
Gussie's back from crusading
mud-dyed, howling, demanding a feast
as if a week's foray were a year on the battlefield.
Tipless tail, kinked midway; perforated ears
and a broad nose chequered with scars:
King Gussie, though often called lesser names,
sprayed supreme, left his scent
and flew his bent flag on foreign blocks.

I think I witnessed his coronation,
one drizzly July day: a circle of twenty or so cats
crowded our backyard, growled and meowed
to their tabby king, who crouched sphinx-still
in the middle, yowling deep and mournful
until one by one they slunk back over fences.

In these days of kitty litter trays and cat cages,
I am proud of our old reprobate's innate ways,
feel privileged to have seen through flyscreen doors
Felis domestica still practising old laws.

Paper Bags

Yasmin and I stood before the whole school
we were five years old, with paper grocery bags
over our heads, almost engulfing our bodies
as they slipped down past our shoulders.
Mine had pointy ears and string whiskers
stuck on with Clag glue; Yasmin's had feathers
and white chalk circles around the eye holes.

Word perfect, we recited *The Owl and the Pussycat*,
Lear's ghost breathing in with us that warm and stuffy
brown paper scent, urging us on when the CO_2
numbed our brains, when our knees knocked
and our hands shook, till we spoke the final line.
Then we danced in the light of the Grade One sun.
And still, I bask in this memory of my first
poetic journey on the pea-green oval of Magill School.

Outcast

for Biggie

We had a cat
the other cats ignored.
She sat and stared
out the window
till we let her out
then she sat and
stared back in.

She sat and stared
at the other cats
as they slept or ate,
sat by their favourite chairs
and stared,
crept along behind them
but never got too close.

They looked the other way
from her green-eyed gaze,
moved away if she tried to play
like we did as kids,
I'm ashamed to say,
from that strange girl at school
who never spoke
but followed us, wanting to play.

The Well

The well greened my thoughts
with emerald moss, ferns,
spiralling down to that
silver-black coin of water.
Sometimes it was a dark throat
that tried to swallow me,
head first, over its lip.

It waited by the casuarina
like a mineshaft ready
to catch curious cats
and careless children.
I wondered at the man with a spade
who made this marvellous hole
a hundred years ago.

Skulls, knives and murder weapons
lurked in the murky sludge
at the bottom of my imagination
where bones slowly turned to gel.
On early summer mornings
scent of mint and cool air rose
from the sweet-breathed mouth.

When bricks began to crumble
parents scolded us for going near.
A galvanised iron lid finally hid
the mossy rim, where history books
say a thirsty donkey once fell in.
And sometimes, late at night,
I'd hear kittens' feeble cries
or a muffled bray.

Invisible Visitor

When the fireside cat arches her back
hackles erect and ears flat,
eyes, wide black holes, see beyond
the realms of human vision.

A chill breeze ruffles curtains
and there's a faint fragrance
of pipe smoke and roast almonds;
the cat growls low, and the light shade
swings silently on its frayed cord –
and nothing will convince me that Uncle Max,
previous owner of this inherited cat,
didn't just pass through the kitchen door.

Shape-shifters

At a certain afternoon hour
my cats curl up:
two new beads
on the tortoiseshell
quilt of autumn leaves.

Later, she moulds or folds
into a jigsaw piece
between my feet
or on my skirt's hammock
hung between warm trunks of flesh
as I write, arched over her.

He stretches like a fur slug
in front of the blow heater
only turning when singeing begins;
or usurps my warm seat
and becomes a big black button,
round, neat, asleep.

When the food tin clinks,
they're two rivers
flowing over my feet
tripping me as they rush
to their bowls, rubbing
and blessing me with purrsong.

Mog or Dog?

You're either a cat or a dog person,
just as you're either into silver or gold,
traits that stick like gum to heels.
You've probably guessed by now
I'm a cat lover – not a hackles-up,
'look-at-me' huffing, sniffing doggie type.

Now…to those of you who are still reading,
my smooth, sleek feline friends,
who know that cats are cleaner, smarter,
and purr along with us in the softness of solitude,
I say, let the dog packs fill the parks,
let their tongues loll as they chase balls and sticks.
We crazy cat people will sit home, lapping up
the blessings of quiet companionship,
stroking the cheek of the velvet moon.

Felis domestica

If you live alone with a cat or cats,
you must accept that at certain hours
your pet will go a-hunting, or a-hiding
curled up alone beneath a secret bush,
perfectly equated to the angle of sun.
If you live alone with a cat or cats,
relaxation and pleasure are yours.
Velvet soft purrs massage your ears,
warm fur strokes your palms back;
until a nibble reminds, it's meal time.

If you live alone with a cat or cats,
you are probably seen as eccentric.
You don't need people – and they know it,
and resent it. Neighbours' tongues yap,
'crazy without a dog for protection'.
I live alone with cats and kids.
Since the divorce, felines saunter boldly,
no one to yell, 'Get that bloody cat out!'
They share my bed, calm and soothe me.
Never a swearword passes their whiskers.

I'm often alone with my friends, my cats:
feisty little gods who lick the hand
that writes, then snatch the pen;
or scratch, contemptuous of a tummy-rub.
We talk, and we fight over heaters at night.
I live alone with cats and part-time kids
but I'm never alone. Bliss on my cheek,
a soft pillow of belly beside my neck.
My new man has stripes and he likes
to bring me gifts of stunned mice. Nice!

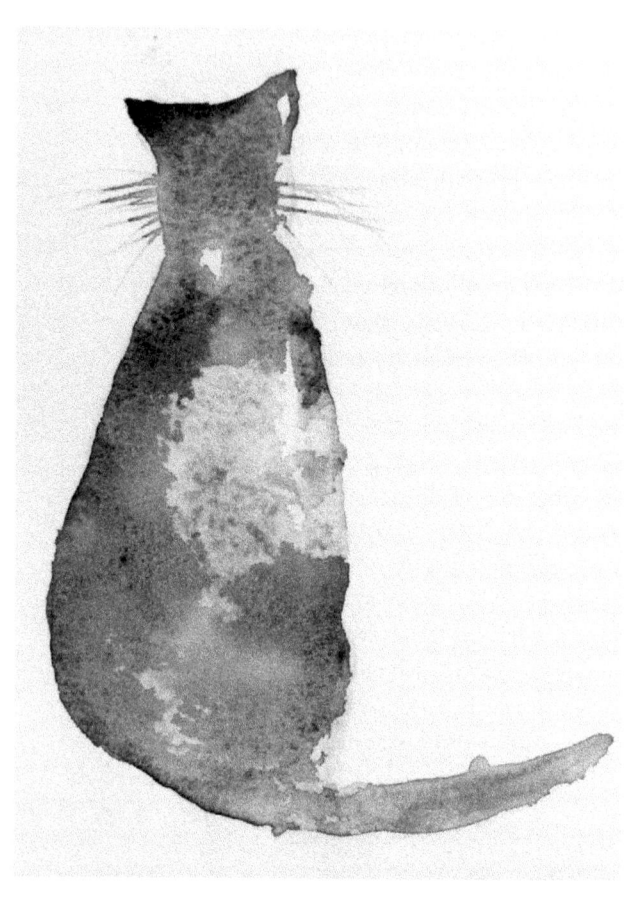

The End

Acknowledgements

The following poems have been previously published:
Imagine the First Cat in England: *The Write Angle*, 2015
Lullabies: *On a moon spiced night*, Wakefield Press, 2004
B C: *On a moon spiced night*, Wakefield Press, 2004
Old Cat: *The School Magazine*, NSW Education Department, 2012
Careers for Cats: *Speak Out*, 2015
Of Mice and Leaves: *The Write Angle*, 2014
Shape-shifting Felines: *Season of a New Heart*, Poets' Corner, 2010
Lunar Cat: *Thread me a button*, Ginninderra Press, 2012
Prowlers: *Knifing the Ice*, Wakefield Press, 2000
Dark Garden: *Poetrix*, 2009
King Gussie: *On a moon spiced night*, Wakefield Press, 2004
Felis Domestica: *Little Book of Cats*, National Library Australia, 2009

I am fortunate to have a talented artistic friend in Angelee Theodoros, who has created many objects of beauty for me over the years. My heartfelt thanks to Angelee for providing the stunning cat portraits in this book. And my sincere thanks to James Ogilvy for his wisdom, friendship and encouragement – and especially for the valuable feedback on *Furry Tales*. Many thanks also to Stephen Matthews and Brenda Eldridge for their indefatigable support to poets and poetry.

Other poetry collections by Jude Aquilina

Knifing the Ice – Wakefield Press, 2000
Friendly Street 24 (co-editor) – Wakefield Press, 2000
On a moon spiced night – Wakefield Press, 2004
WomanSpeak (with Louise Nicholas) – Wakefield Press, 2009
Season of a New Heart (co-editor) – Poets' Corner, 2009
Thread me a button (with Joan Fenney) – Ginninderra Press, 2012
Ship Tree – Picaro Press, 2012
Tadpoles in the Torrens (editor) – Wakefield Press, 2013
Beauty and the Breast – Garron Publishing, 2013

The author and Mr Piecroft
(Photo by Annette Willis)

www.ingramcontent.com/pod-product-compliance
Ingram Content Group UK Ltd.
Pitfield, Milton Keynes, MK11 3LW, UK
UKHW022209230426
12048UKWH00016BA/738